Hiding from
and Other H(

Michael Potts

Table of Contents

Scene Splice to Kubrick's *The Shining*

Danny takes his three-wheeler down
the infinite hall where parallel lines
never end in a wall. And there they are,
the murdered girls, dressed in their Sunday
best. They say *We want you to play
with us forever and ever and ever,*
as the scene shifts to their dead
bodies lying on the floor, pink fabric
splotched with red blood, and the voice
in Danny's head telling him to remember
that Mr. Hallorann said *It's not real.*
But when Danny goes to bed that night
two girls' voices whisper in his ear,
But we are real, Danny.

A Mystic Meets God

A mystic leaves the body,
seeks to find God
and ask for an answer
to life's meaning.
He floats in space,
prays for grace.
Stars, darkness pass,
and at the edge
of a black hole,
gravity stealing
gas from a nearby
star, a voice calls
from the distance.
The mystic knows
he's attained--God
appears, a great eye
black as night,
nihilistic dark that robs
souls of any feeling
but despair—blind,
uncaring, its mouth fixed
in a constant scream,
and madness
its source
of being. The mystic wakes,
walks to an open window,
leaps into icy air, despair
unredeemed by death.

Black Moths

swarm into the shape
of a bearded man
whose moth-mouth moves
as he speaks. *I'm Jesus*
and you haven't obeyed
me. You drink whisky,
dance with lascivious
lust, take my name in vain
and I say, *If you're Jesus,*
raise my wife from the dead
and he says, *It is written,*
Thou shalt not tempt
the Lord thy God so I take
my double-barreled twelve gauge
and fill his face with shot.
Moth guts spatter,
body scatters,
survivors fly away.
I take a sip
of bourbon and walk
to a square dance

where I find my wife,
hold her, dance.
She asks, *Why did*
you bring me back
only to let me die
again? When I try
to reply, her clothes
give way, collapse
to the floor, disappear
into a black moth cloud.

Buzzard Talk

High in the sky I circle
my prey, your dying scent
driving me. I wait for you
to fall, crawl, collapse.
Meanwhile, I fly, study
your dust-caked face,
eager to eat delicacies
beneath. Finally
you crash, stay still—
I dive, sense your heart's
silence before I savor
your dead, delicious flesh.

Cadaver Lab, Physician Assistant Program

Inside the cadaver lab, block walls
gleam white, cold air races from vents,
formaldehyde scent. Steel tables hide
half-dissected bodies. Students enter,
chat, uncover, cut the core of human
flesh. It's the third week of the semester,
head and brain off. A student finds a half face,
a flap of flayed skin, lifts it
to the window. Blue sky shines through
empty eye sockets. *We're done with that,*
says the teacher, *throw it out.* Someone
flings it into a bag. At another body,
a student clips the ribs, lifts
the coffin-like cage, exposing lungs
nesting the heart, snug in its pericardial
sac. The teacher explains the phrenic
nerve--*cut it, a person's dead—here's*
the thymus, atrophied with age; there's
the trachea--touch the cartilage rings--
he goes on, listing and describing,
as if dignity had a human face
that could be peeled and lifted off.

Classic Body

She leers at his
muscular chest,
his patterned pecs,
his flat abdomen.
She strokes his face
under the hole
in his forehead
left by her .38,
his body pale
as the Greek statues
she so admires.

Cleaning Prey on Thanksgiving Day

Daddy's great
at cleaning—
he cuts off
the head,
lets blood drain,
deftly pulls
skin aside,
exposing red
muscle.

He slits,
belly to neck—
out pours guts,
liver, lungs,
and the heart
which I take,
try to squeeze
a beat,
but it won't.

Thanksgiving's great
I say. Daddy smiles.
Your cousin Earl
came late, he says,
but made it
just in time—
lean with enough fat
to flavor the steaks.
My mouth waters.

Whisper of the Sea

I watch an old Twilight Zone episode—
someone whispers the meaning of life
and all who hear go mad. Now, past
my middle years, I fear the answer's
coming soon, that it will be Nein,
Nihil, Nada, like Stephen Crane's sea
that doesn't give a damn, that sea
I'm standing in as waves wash
my waist. I ask why I shouldn't go
deeper, let the depths take me—
instead I turn around, walk towards
shore, decide to linger as long as Fate
allows me to stay out of the Abyss,
waiting as Nothingness gnaws my flesh,
claws my mind, digests meaning.

Conjuration

The Mayan symbol for to conjure is a hand grasping a fish.
From watery chaos cold demons come
when I call. My spirit, entranced,
holds them fast. *Cause my enemies*
to fall, I command. The devils obey,
hooked by charms, reeled by spells
conjured from the depths of hell.
When the demons have done their deeds,
my enemies defeated, their hearts
gifts for the gods, I'll cast the devils
back into the nightmare place,
that endless ocean space, deep
beyond bounds, older than the gods,
colder than the icy depths of the sea.

The Blood-Dark Sea

Talons claw a sailor's brain—
pain beyond bearing shoots
through his head like a flame tipped
knife, mind pulled apart
bit by bit until he falls dead,
bloodshot eyes open, unseeing—
The captain tries to turn the ship around
and flee full steam ahead, the sound
and stench of the tentacled thing
attacking, haunting them with dark
dreams, driving them to scream their last
breaths, their deaths logged in the non-
Euclidean mind behind the skull-like face
and knowing eyes—the sailors cry,
go mad, die, their ship left to float,
alone, a rusted hulk, ghost lost
on the blood-dark sea.

Cuneiform

The old man's fingers touch the tablet's grooves,
cuneiform cut into ancient clay. His office—dark
except his desk lit by a florescent lamp that's
focused on slashed letters and a centered crude
carving, a creature with death's head face,
its squid-like body's arms reaching, probing.
The old man swivels his chair away from light,
away from the clay with eyes that seem to stare—
then something wet, slick, cold touches the nape
of his neck, a kiss too obscene for this world.

Portal

Sunlight forces its way through spaces
between logs. Oak shade shifts in wind,
shimmering the dust-filled floor, forming
an unholy alliance of light and dark.
Planks from the partly-collapsed roof
rot outside the door, the remaining beams
joining at odd angles that feel obscene.
A hiss scratches the air—a vulture guards
the ruined fireplace, sounds escaping
from its beak like voices of devoured dead.
Its feathers flap, it flies towards my face,
hovers, eyes shifting to focus on mine.
Like sunlit grains of sand they blind,
but I find my hands paralyzed, unable to block
the light. Infinite stars go blank, scratched out
by tentacles growing from malevolence
reaching through vulture eyes, stretching,
penetrating my brain, haunting my dreams.

Red in Tooth and Tentacle

Slack flesh stretches
across an oversized skull,
mouth a straight line,
eyes slicing souls
into fragments, leaving
bodies barely alive,
minds insane—
and the Ancient One
doesn't care
about the pain
he causes, indifferent
as Fate, beyond
all love and hate.

R'lyeh

Beneath the sea R'lyeh sleeps
in stones that wait like bones
to be enfleshed—and Great Cthulhu
rests, lost in dreams, patient
until the stars are right and light
leaves the world forever.

Azathoth

At the center of all things
lies the no-thing, Azathoth
the Blind, the Idiot, without
mind, whose form unfolds
dimensions into formlessness.
God anencephalic, whose
meaningless wailing haunts—
do not search, knowledge
seeker; do not listen, music
lover—or else your own screams
won't end with your death.

The Lake

The water sank a thousand feet
down through broken clay
walls and limestone mixed
with iron from an ancient
meteorite, whose flight stopped
ten thousand years ago.
On the water's surface, a boat
floats—inside, an old man waits
for union, to be no longer one,
but joined with what's below,
the being to whom he's bowed,
the thing that feeds him dreams
and eats his mind.

Dance of the Gods

Bodies writhe, their heads misshapen,
some missing—on one neck, a lidless eye,
forever blind. Legs prance like ponies,
disappear into some unknown dimension,
appear again as flutes pipe a schizophrenic
tune—gods infernal encircle the universe's
center, where dwells Azathoth the Idiot—
and The Others, lost in madness, dance.

Nyarlathotep

When I died, my body lying,
doctors squeezing my heart,
you ripped me away,
and I flew through
an open gate into a void—
I stopped. No space,
no time—blackness.
I awakened. The horror of your
non-Euclidian form pulled me
inside and I knew you—

Nyerlathotep, Keeper of Worlds,
Guardian of Dimensions.
You sent me to the city
of dreams—misshapen creatures
full of mind-ears probed me,
drew out sanity, left behind
a broken shell—
I flew back from hell,
back through nowhere,
back into my body,
and the gate clicked closed.

Yog-Sothoth

Candles lit in my dark office,
light flickering on my varnished
desk. I repeat the mantra
Yog-Sothoth, Yog-Sothoth—
wormwood incense rises,
twists into knots, disappears.
I'm spreading out, body stretched,
filling the room, dispersing
though walls and into infinite space.
Heatless cold freezes my flesh--
worlds stuffed with life, some
earthlike, others with reptiles
ensouled, snakes full of venom
and malice, silicon stones
who say *I think, therefore, I am*—
I pass through dimensions beyond
time, and I shut my eyes against
insanity—and realize Yog-Sothoth is—
all spaces, times, the apeiron,
infinite coldness uncaring.

Cthulhu's Harvest

Through threads of time and dream
Great Cthulhu waits—above, stars
stay the same until the change
when R'lyeh rises from the sea
and Death no longer lies beneath
the Deep, devoid of light.
Then the High Priest springs,
the Old Ones rule the Earth again,
cleaving body from soul, searing
minds to madness, sowing demon
seeds that scatter order into chaos,
grow until they drain the last
drops of meaning from existence.

Worship

A fire centers a clearing's circle
edged by a grove of oak
and birch. Tentacled masks
hide faces, shadowed legs
prance like twitching matchsticks.
Worshippers dance hand-in-hand,
crying phrases only they understand—
then silence. The sacrifice arrives,
tied to a post. The revelers make way,
the post is pushed into red clay.
Ph'nglui mglw'nafh Cthulhu R'lyeh
wgah'nagl fhtagn—the dancers
chant and wait—then from below
clawed fingers reach to touch
the victim's head, his soul
split into chaos, his mouth yielding
screams until the claws close
shut, skull pieces dripping,
brain slipping onto dew-strewn
leaves, and Great Cthulhu
falls back into the beyond,
back into that city R'lyeh,
back to his throne where he
rests, dead but not dead,
waiting to wake once more.

Considering

The tornado turns, moves
toward the Ford pickup,
the man inside trying to floor
it, but the monster closes,
its maw opening over the man's
head. *Go away*, he says, hoping
somehow that thing can think.
He falls, covers his head
but the twister hovers
as if sleeping
or pondering—
the wind dies down
for a moment, then blows
faster. The thing's dark
mouth narrows to a frown
and mouths the word *No*.

Consummation

Bags in hand, the man leaves
to pry his future bride
from her father's prison.
Night without light, absent
moon—-the man, encased
in fear, walks, his hope
quenching thirst, his desire,
hunger. He reaches their chosen
place, steps between graves,
meets his beloved. He says
his private vows, how he'll be
part of her forever and she
of him. Then he screams
as she consummates his promise,
her lower jaw dropping
to her chest, her teeth knife
blades, her fingers scalpels.
She shreds his flesh and dines,
no longer fearing her father's
wrath, her lover's body
joined as one with hers.

Crows on a Power Line

Crows caw, sitting on a power line,
black bird shapes against blue
bruising the sky. Suddenly one
flies high into the air, searching
for prey——he dives like a bomber,
and it's some time before he rises,
sated with the flesh and blood
he's gorged——unlike us, who kill
and kill again, insatiable.

Bagging Prey

I spot him with headlights
on my pickup. He freezes,
eyes gleaming as I raise
my deer rifle, aim, pop him
between the eyes. He drops,
lights out, with a thud.
Takes a while to skin
the animal, lots of fat
to cut through--still enough
lean meat to fill the freezer—
I'll keep the visceral stuff, too.
Though eating it will be bad
for my heart, I don't see why
good meat should go to waste.
I reckon it will take about a year
to eat my dear
husband, best
meat I ever had.

Dissecting the Heart

The student's hands hold
the woman's heart, lift it
from her unribbed chest, set
it down to dissect, knife
hovering like steel wings.
It pierces the pericardial
sac, slitting tissue away,
exposing naked myocardium,
formaldehyde brown, decay
delayed for science's sake.
Slicing through the septum,
he splits the heart in half,
exposing atria, ventricles,
cordae tendenae, cusps
of valves: tricuspid, mitral
pulmonary, aortic. Inserting
a gloved finger, he divides
the bishop's miter, forcing
bloodless cusps apart,
finger flicking flaps,
out-in, out-in, out-in.
Studying the specimen, he finds
a scar of an old infarction,
heart attack written on the apex,
spilled ink splattered on a clean
page. He looks down at the woman's
legs, gangrenous black, and remembers
his grandmother gasping for air.

Drama Queen Karma

She said she'd worked
as a nurse in Kenya
but lied.

Then she said her heart had stopped
and she saw her dead mother—
another lie.

She told me her sister
had hanged herself—
a lie

and after she died St. Peter said
You're going to heaven—
he lied.

Empty Grave

Passing the graveyard where my twin lies,
driving on a dirt road at 2 a.m.
on my way home to wife and cats, tears in my eyes
from feeling alone, I wonder why I'm
driving down that dirt road at 2 a.m.,
thinking of the half that's six feet under. I'm tired
of feeling alone, wondering why I'm
caring so much about a stillbirth, why I'm mired
in grief, pondering why he's six feet under. I'm tired
of trying to live up to a dead child,
but I go on, grieving over a stillborn brother. I'm mired
in emotional mud, heart buried by a pile
of pain, driving on a dirt road at 2 a.m.,
passing the graveyard where my brother lies
dead, wood box and cartilage decayed, not a gram
left in the grave where my dead brother lies.

To Meet You Again

Night's chill cuts my skin
like a straightedge. The heat
of your breath had touched
my ear in bed, your whisper
saying, *Come here*--and I am,
boots tramping fresh snow,
flashlight's beam slicing
through ice fog. Falling flakes
prick my face like God's
arrows, but I reach your grave

and you're there, standing,
gesturing for my embrace
which I freely give--but my
arms slip through icy air,
your dark hair merging
into the blackness beyond.

Your lips move--I try to read
the words--*love, why, hurt,
kill*--and with a thrill I remember
the fight, a kitchen knife
in my hands, the forward motion
of my arm. *Forgive* I gasp—
but you're gone. Wind swirls
around me, a whirlwind of snow
engulfs me, and I wait, my love,
to meet you again.

Haunted Justice

The old family home stands alone,
deserted as the woods in which I walk.
Stone steps sit like sentinels
guarding the front door. Shadow
streaks from maples slice the stones
like knives. With pounding pulse
I climb the wooden floors that creak
like cracked bones of memory.
The bedroom's still intact where
at six I watched my father take a knife
and carve my mother's head clean off
her neck. My father went to jail
and died there of a painless stroke.
That's not right, I say aloud and mourn
the lack of justice, my mother unavenged.

I shut my eyes, open them to find
my mother's face forming in the space
where she died. Her body coalesces
and her severed head shifts onto her neck--
a neat fit--and in her hand a carving knife.
Then my father appears whole, face torn
by fear as my mother separates his body
from his head. The scene repeats again,
again--I'm pleased to see my father's hell,
well of vengeance infinitely sweet.

In Hell

If only hell
were flames,
sulfur stench,
demon whips
lashing my bare back.

Time I can't count here,
a place beyond years
but not beyond tears.

Guilt walks embodied—
my wife's accusing eyes
after my third affair,
my oldest son I struck
for wetting the bed,
the boss I embezzled—
images always haunting,
never leaving
since I lack eyes to close,
ears to stop. Again,
again they come,
those I hurt,
three-dimensional nightmares
conscience-fed.

Leave!
I shout,
but no one hears—
alone I'm pierced
by accusers' arrows,
knowing they strike
true.

Hiding from the Reaper

Home from work, I wrap myself
in a comforter on the living room
couch, roll it into a cocoon.

Soon I'll fall asleep and hope
to dream about anything other
than death. Seven restless nights
I've dreamed of drowning
in a dirty creek, of knives piercing
my chest, of tumbling on sharp stones
that split my head, and I wake up
screaming in bed. *Some peace,*
please, I pray with closed eyes,
hearing the hollow thud of my heart
slowing. An hour later, awake,
I stare at the mottled surface
of the comforter under my head.

A sliver of light peeks
through an opening for air.
I'm afraid to move, hoping
the skeleton feet following
will pass me by.

Homecoming

At home, his wife
kisses children goodnight--
Daddy will be back
tomorrow. She crawls
into a cold bed, wraps a quilt
around her head. *Another*
business trip, I'm sorry,
her husband had said—

she believed
and dreamed
his touch.

Away from home, he touches
a costly breast, thrusts
himself into two thousand
dollars of betrayal—

but when he comes
so does a clot
that blocks the blood
to his heart.

Three heartbeats remain
in his life.

One—
his daughter dreams
of a tea party
with Daddy.

Two—
his son dreams
of playing in mud
with Daddy.

Three—
his wife masturbates
to his photo.
When she comes
he dies.

Canning Instructions

Place quart and pint
canning jars, seals and lids
in pan of hot water.
In large cooking pot,
pour a gallon of vinegar,
a gallon of water.

Add a half cup of salt.
Bring to a boil.

Place jar on potholder.
Place heart in jar.
Fill jar with boiling solution.
Use plastic knife to clear bubbles.

Remember that women's hearts
are smaller; they might fit
in the pint jars, unless the woman
was an athlete. Men's though,
usually require quart jars.

Carefully place seal over jar.
Screw top on snugly.

Mandible

I bought a human mandible—
couldn't afford a skull—
a reminder that Death's head
hides behind my face.

The jawbone—yellow,
with three half-decayed teeth—
a real bargain
at thirty-five dollars.

I take the dead bone,
playfully spin its half-grin
with my index finger.

Then cold breath brushes
and I wonder whether Death
has come to de-flesh
my skin and muscle.

I turn around—a woman
stands, her stare a burning
glare, and I drop the jawbone.

Her lower jaw lies slack,
a formless flap: she opens
her mouth, her voice watery.

That's mine.

She's right.
I give her the mandible
which she snaps
into her jaw—
she fades
into nothing.

I glance at the space
where I'd set
the mandible
but all that remains—
a receipt.

Night Before Bypass

All I can think about is the Black
& Decker jigsaw and its surgeon.
I imagine the grind and grate as the saw
slices its way through my breastbone.

I overhear the surgeon, who stands
in the hall—he talks about his wife,
a fight last night, approaching divorce.
*Don't know how the hell I'll make
it through surgery tomorrow.*

I imagine the surgeon sawing—
mind left behind at the office
of his attorney, emotions sawed
into heart-red fragments. A slip
of anger in his heart is all
it would take to slip into mine.

When he operates, I hope he leaves
his heart out of it.

Nihilism

Despair darker than death's blankness
haunts the man at two a.m., the time
he thinks about his extinction,
consciousness wiped out like a smudge
of dirt by a cloth. Sitting up, throat
tightening, he glances at the clock
by his bed, red letters passing time,
marking dead moments, the present's
constant murder by the past. The man
gasps air that suddenly seems thin,
grasps at meaning that hangs on a cliff's
edge, but it falls as he lunges, disappears
as if never existing at all.

Old Photo, Cracker Barrel, Oak Ridge, Tennessee

A woman rests serene in an oval frame.
Long dark hair hangs, two strands draped
over her right shoulder, an oversized
thickness of braided hair drooping her left.
Loose folds of a white dress hide
her torso. Her pupils—fixed.
Does she stare and think of a lost
lover? Or is she dead, propped
for a photo, mouth frozen
in an enigmatic frown, lips sewn shut,
silent for some final pose?

Old Woman Alone, Reading *A Picture of Dorian Gray*

Her fingers loosen. The book slips
to the carpet. She starts awake,
scratches her face, flakes of dead
skin falling on her pants. Brushing
them off, she pulls a hand mirror
from her purse and views a sea—
ancient, stormy—of wrinkles
except for the smooth, pink skin
where she'd scratched before.
She takes a razor blade, removes
the rest, head to toe, then admires
her young face, firm breasts, flat
belly, before she falls asleep.
Tomorrow someone will find
her flayed body, bloody skin
curls littering the floor.

Orpheus Looking Back

He couldn't wait.
The one task Hades asked—
Beauty turned him back—

Eurydice dressed in white,
a bride pulled from death
by Beauty of another kind.

She fades into the passionless
shades, her lover doomed
to join her soon, their deaths
like the ends of all loves,
killed by cares, anger, affairs—

until finally lovers look back
to find Hades's face, patient
as Fate, waiting with open arms.

Potter's Field

The old man's cane slips on a rock—
he starts to slide but breaks his fall.
Stumbling ahead, tracks guide him
toward the liquor store. But he's lost
track of time—the moon descends
below cedar branches. It's dark
and the man's tired, so he lies down,
cane by his side, a cross tie
his pillow. Too late he hears
the whistle and he sits up—
there's a final scream,
an obliterated face,
a body carved into a head,
a trunk, two severed legs—
he'll rest unmissed, unmourned,
in the Potter's Field.

Scaling and Cleaning

He scrapes scales away,
cuts off tail fins, cleans
out guts. The rest—
the female face,
the breasts—
he throws back.

Shoeshine Man

dabs wax on a paper towel,
rubs dull surfaces,
takes a brush,
scuffs back and forth,
brings out shine.

The same ritual
every month
for ten years—
first, his dress shoes,
then black walking shoes,
finally his wife's
skull.

Skin Deep

Someone had cared for the car—
the noon sun shined bright
on its black paint, its windshield
washed by recent rain. I pull open
the door, sit on a seat too large
for my small body, reach, touch
my fingertips to the steering wheel,
pretend to drive. Later, outside,
I crack the hood, take a peek
before I lose my grip, my hands
slipping out just in time. I stand
still, shocked at what I've seen—
a rusted radiator, the engine
busted, the battery leaking dark
liquid that looks like clotted blood.
Sixty years pass. I stand, look down
at my muscled chest, molded abs—
I feel my face, skin smooth, firm
as a forty-year-old's. Three years
from seventy, with the heart
of someone thirty—and cancer
feeding on my lungs, my liver,
leaching my insides away.

Skipped Beats

One December afternoon, Death paid
me a visit. Came right into my living room
as I watched TV in the rocking chair.

He crept behind me, turned into mist,
and I breathed him into my lungs,
where he stood, his legs flanking
my heart, a cold body inside my warm
flesh. He took a rope out of his black bag,
and jumped rope over my heart. *Slam!*
Heart struck my chest from the inside.
Death kept jumping; my heart skipped,
three more times, with death taunting
and teasing me as my heart halted,
then lived again.

Got up, ran into my room,
grabbed a stethoscope, pressed it to my chest.
Death laughed, a child taunting a playmate,
put his rope away and played hop scotch—

little dyings, pauses too long before the next
beat. Tried to forget, drove to Wal-Mart,
hiding from death with other forgetful folks,
trying to bury it in routine. And then,
strangely, bored with me, he exited
while I washed in the Men's Room.

Stalker [form: Cyhydedd Hir]

My ex-lover lied—
she claimed that I tried
to force her. She cried,
calling the cops
and I stayed in jail
three nights, then made bail.
I found her but failed
to make her stop.
She turned me in, claimed
I forced her again.
With nothing to gain
I got away.
So now I'm driving
to nowhere, trying
to find some meaning
for which to pray.
My '68 truck
running on luck
gets stuck on a mud
road in the wild.
I'm alone with nowhere
as home and there's no
town for ten miles.
Above, the moon's face
mocks, saying, *Don't
take time to pray:
today you'll die.*
I walk in the dark,
talk to the space
that stalks me like a lie.

Steel Drum

The woman burns the dead man's sheets
in a rusty steel drum. Blackened fabric
flakes fly into a gray sky. The sun
begins to set, but the fire burns—yellow,
orange, red—finishing the final remnants
of her dead husband she'd wrapped
inside—his skull, now black, grinning
a greeting through a hole in the drum.

Happy with Grandma

The little girl gazes at her grandmother's
body lying in a casket, the old woman dressed
in her blue Sunday dress, her face glowing
pink under lamplight. She seems alive
and the girl grasps her grandmother's icy
hand, drops it, screams. Her mother pulls
her away but she wants to stay—she stares
at her grandmother's unmoving chest, still
as the chapel air—then she sees it rise.
The girl leaps inside the casket—the lid
closes, her head rests between her grandmother's
breasts, her ear near the silent, dead heart.
Breathe, Granny, breathe she says
but Granny won't. People pry open
the lid, pull the girl's arms
from Granny's neck. At home
that night, the girl dreams of being
trapped in Granny's grave, feeling breaths,
cold as death, hiss through Granny's
blue lips. And the girl thinks she'll stay
with Granny, play games forever.
There she'll be happy.

The Straw Man

stands in a corn patch,
a sentry at attention
watching for invading
children, ready to digest
their tiny bodies, drink
their blood, spit out
their bones. When
the corn is gone
the wind arrives,
blows the man
to strands of straw
that float to earth,
decay—then summer
grasses die, dry,
form the man again.

Uncle Clark's Change

When Uncle Clark came home he said,
I've turned into a monster. We didn't
know what to do—we surely doubted
him until he chewed Cousin Molly
and spit out her skull—then we had a clue
somethin' weren't quite right,
so we sat outside Uncle Clark's bedroom
and the old fool opened the door—damned
if he weren't wearin' a wolf's head
and eight-inch claws. We ran like hell—
Charlie asked if we should call the law
on Clark but I said, *We gotta put*
a silver bullet in his head but Junior—
he's real smart—said, *No, shoot him*
in his heart so we melted
some of Charlie's silver fillings
and made a bullet, which I put in my
.22 special and plugged ole' Clark
in his chest but damned if that shot
didn't miss the heart and I think I broke
the land speed record for rednecks.

Waiting

He hangs, feet first,
in the smokehouse.
Headless, gutless,
the hog waits,
without worry,
to become dinner.

Wish Granted

As a child I wanted to fly:
I'd flap my arms in brisk wind,
praying it would lift me
into the sky where
I'd play with a flock of quail,
touch a cloud's edge,
visit town ten miles away
to buy a Snickers bar.
Now, my wish fulfilled,
my fragments fly toward town,
blown by superheated breath
of a mushroom cloud.

At the Trash Pile

Billy met a boy named
Sonny Blake, who said
he'd be Billy's friend
for life. They played
with broken glass
from old beer bottles
and jars of salad dressing,
cut each other's hands
to become blood brothers
and then they walked
to the top of the hill
where an old black Ford
from the forties lay
abandoned. They got in,
shut the door, pretended
to drive and Billy said,
I used to play in this car
with Granddaddy but
he's been dead two years
and Sonny said, *I know him.*
He's a nice man, and Billy
couldn't stop screaming.

Basement Door

You tiptoe to the basement door,
snap off the hook and push
it open. Below you the floor
is covered with dust.
Now you fear to take a step
because you know you'll see a ghost
staring up the steps,
who wants to make you fall
and join its world behind
the dirt-encrusted wall.
Then you'll be a ghost yourself
and you'll try to scare
the boy or girl who opens
the door that leads nowhere.

Clown

Your parents take you to the fair
to see a circus clown.
Morty's my name he says.
I'll make a Snoopy dog.
He blows up a balloon, twists it
into the shape of a dog.
With a pen he draws eyes, nose,
mouth and ears. He gives
you Snoopy and you laugh.
Then Morty says *I'll make you*
one more thing. You clap your hands,
say, *Great!* and watch the clown's
kind white-painted face. He finishes
your toy, hands it to you.
Two black eye holes stare you down,
Black dots make the nose, the mouth's
a toothy grin—a skull. As you drop
the twisted toy and flee, Morty says
Remember me—next time I'll visit you.

Empty House

When the candle burns out
inside your jack-o-lantern,
ghosts float through the ground
into the air until they find
the pumpkin's hollow eyes
and open mouth. They fly
inside and dance the sticky
floor until dawn. They leave
with a sigh you hear
at five a.m. You think
it's only wind—but it's not.

It Only Wants to Play

Do you think if you walk
through a graveyard in daylight
you'll be safe? You're wrong—
some ghosts are brave, and wander
out of their graves, wanting to see
the light of day and remember
what it was like to be a child and play—
these ghosts stand behind you
and watch. Sometimes they
crave what you have so much
that they wave their ghostly arms
beside your ears. If you listen,
you might hear their whispery
voices say, *Come play with us.*

June Bug

When the june bugs come out this summer,
you might consider catching one and tying
a string to a back leg and watch it fly around
your head. My advice is, *Don't.* I once knew
a boy who made a june bug his toy, but forgot
about there being more than one. His bug escaped,
buzzed its fellow bugs, who flew together
to form a wall. The boy saw them coming
and ran—too late—the bugs caught him,
surrounded him in a whirlwind. His sister
found his skull and a few rib bones. Now if
a june bug flies into your path, it's fine
to pick it up, admire the green gleam of its belly
in sunlight—but be sure to let it go.

Kidnapper

Don't play too late at night
around an old tree.
When branches turn black
in dying light, you'd better get
inside your house. If you don't,
a branch will pull you up
and hide you in the leaves.
Your mom and dad won't find
you before the tree sucks you
inside its trunk. From there
you'll grow as a branch,
your fingers and toes turning
to leaves that whisper in the breeze.

Night Reading

Don't you know that reading a scary story
at night brings the monsters to life?
When the lights are out and you've read
that story about ghosts or zombies or worse,
you try to walk down the hall to your bedroom,
that's when you feel the beasts are real,
a whiff of cold breath on the back of your neck,
clawed hands clutching your shoulders.

Snakes in a Pipe

You hear water gurgle down the drain
through pipes to an unseen place—
but you, girls and boys—you know
that snakes live there—two-headed
snakes, deformed snakes with tiny legs
or stumps, snakes with three-inch fangs.
They're born in the sewer, migrate
to pipes, prepare to crawl to your sink,
drawn by the smell of children. So wash
your hands but watch for snakes,
and if you see a head or two
burst through the drain and stare,
beware its bite and go away,
and call your mom or dad to stay
and take care of that drainpipe snake.

The Skull

When you're in the store before Halloween,
look at the white plastic skulls gleaming
on the shelves. Pick one up, find a mirror.
Place the skull next to your face. But know
this: that under your thin skin sits something
that grins even when you frown, smiles
when you scowl. Run your fingers down
your jawbone to your chin, up to your lips;
pull them back, get a good look
at your teeth. Imagine your gums gone,
your skin flaked off, your muscles
invisible. Examine the remains.
Does your skull look the same as the fake?

Toy Eater

One morning you'll wake up and find a hole
in your favorite toy and wonder how
it got there—but I will tell you why—
I cast a spell upon a doll who creeps
into your room at night and feeds on
your toys. She takes a tiny knife and cuts
a hole to pluck and widen at she eats
the toy from inside out—but you're asleep.
It's okay—she leaves before you wake.

Under the Covers

I wake up, feeling snug and safe
under the covers. No bad dreams
or monsters harm me. Here,
darkness is comfort, warming me
like an extra blanket. I open my eyes,
soak up the black, breathe it in.
But then I feel the skin of my hands
untouched by fabric. I move them
but they stop at something solid.
Finally I pull them from beneath
the unknown barrier, reach up to find
a surface sleek, smooth as polished pine.

Monsters

Deep under your bed,
under the floor,
underground,
lie things that creep.
When you're asleep,
they claw their way up,
break through the floor,
cut the carpet.
Then they climb
bedsprings, slice
through your mattress
with sharp teeth
and hide
under your sheets,
hob-knobbing
around your feet
until you awaken
not knowing
they're there.

Beating Death

I lie on my side underneath a large oak.
Standing stones surround me like approaching
Death. But he won't get here today, to this place
of graves. I told him he wouldn't steal me away
early, like my twin brother, torn from life
two hours after birth, blood mucking his lungs
until he drowned. Once is enough, Dark Angel.
I lie in your territory, lie here waiting to break
your skinny hand. I know one day you'll take me,
but not yet, not until I'm old with hair white
as your bleached bones. Then God will raise
me and my brother, and in the light of day
that's never night we'll play over your grave.
I'll dance to the sounds of your xylophone ribs,
my brother beating out a rhythm with your arm-bone
sticks, as we crush the rest of you with our feet.

Sifting

My hands sift your pink
aureole field,
fingers dancing
on the plateau
of your creamy
pale breasts.

Your skin,
brown in dim
light, fades
into cool air.
With my arms I

try to pluck you back,
but you're gone.
I smash the night
with my fist, weep

as I close the box
holding the dust
of your bones.

Tough Love

She releases her grip
on the serrated steak knife
pinning her husband's
neck to the floor,
and ever-so-softly asks him,
*Was that woman
worth the cost?*

As his last gasp gurgles
into the air,
she kisses his lips,
walks to a drawer
filled with love
letters, jewelry,
small stuffed animals,
anniversary gifts,
and lifts one
at a time, pressing it
between her breasts.

Hate is love held
in abeyance.

It Comes in Twos

The first time
the boy thought deeply
about death,
he was six.
He'd seen
a dead rabbit
beside the highway,
and wondered
what would happen
if he himself
were hit.

When he turned eight,
his great-grandfather lay,
wearing a black suit
and tie,
in a steel casket
at Miller's Funeral Home.
The dead man's lips
turned up in a smirk.

At ten
his parents drove
past a wreck.
The boy looked out
the rear window
of their Chevy
at a bloody sheet
and felt a chill.

He was twelve,
hunting quail,
the day his dad
collapsed,
turned pale

as paper,
the eyes
rolling back.

Two weeks later,
the boy masturbated
for the first time.

Tease

You, who breathed life into Adam,
removed his rib to create Eve,
why do you leave me those without
breath, family and friends sickled
by Death, and from You, no trickle
of comfort--only a vague hope
of a land too wonderful to understand—
dead abstractions never helped
a soul lost on a maple leaf ground,
old rotted leavings of life. My un-being,
St. John of the Cross's dark night
when World's Light hides in a nest
of kidnapped lives and dead abandoned
eggs. Hope of eternal life lost,
Death's sickle slicing a silver cord.
Darkness comes, bringing the worst—
death-dreams, screams from an abyss
fading like a train whistle. Sleep, relief,
dawn. You reappear with Morning Light
as your guest. You pull me back, breathe
warmth onto my face and I revive
to drive Despair away until tonight
when You come at two a.m. Then
You touch my shoulder with your hand
and I, awakened, sense You flee again.

About the Author:

Michael Potts is the author of *End of Summer*, a novel about loss and recovery of faith, published by WordCrafts Press in 2011. His poetry chapbook, *From Field to Thicket*, won the 2006 Mary Belle Campbell Poetry Book Award of the North Carolina Writers' Network. His creative nonfiction essay, "Haunted," won the 2006 Rose Post Creative Nonfiction Award from the same organization. He is a 2007 graduate of The Writer's Loft program at Middle Tennessee State University and a 2007 graduate of the Odyssey Writing Workshop. A native of Smyrna, Tennessee, he now serves as Professor of Philosophy at Methodist University in Fayetteville, North Carolina. He, his wife, Karen, and their three cats, Frodo, Pippin, and Rosie, live in Linden, North Carolina.

Webpage: http://www.michael-potts.com
Twitter: http://www.twitter.com/Cthulhu77
Facebook: http://www.facebook.com//michael.potts3
My Literary Blog: http://michaelpotts.livejournal.com
My General Blog: http://gratiaetnatura.wordpress.com

Lightning Source UK Ltd.
Milton Keynes UK
UKHW022129030620
364382UK00018B/310